Zayn
Levels Up

Written by Maisie Chan

Illustrated by Francesca Ficorilli

Collins

1 Power cut

Zayn had been playing his game all morning.

He was stuck on Level 49. To level up, he had to hit square targets without crossing red beams.

3

To make things harder, there were burning discs to avoid. The discs were thrown by the Level 50 gatekeeper, a fearsome bear.

"I'm almost at Level 50!" Zayn shouted.

All of a sudden, the screen went dark.
Zayn pressed his controller. Nothing happened.

"It's taken me a month to get this far!"
Zayn jumped up. "Mum! Power cut!"

2 The visitor

Something tapped Zayn's shoulder. He turned and blinked in shock. Was this a nightmare?

In front of him stood a life-sized bear.
The gatekeeper was in his room!

"Don't be scared," said the bear, towering over Zayn.

"But ..." Zayn stared. "You're supposed to be in there," he spluttered, pointing to the screen.

The bear sighed. "I'm always in that game, protecting the gateway. I want to help others instead."

Zayn's mouth fell open. "Can you help me get to Level 50?"

"Yes! First, you need to learn to avoid the burning discs," the bear explained. "Come with me."

As Zayn stepped outside, something flew above his head.

"Look out!" shouted the bear.

Zayn picked the disc up, frowned and then threw it back.

For the rest of the morning, Zayn leapt, spun and took cover as the red disc came at him.

"Now, targets!" The bear found the toy bow and arrow set Zayn got for his birthday.

The bear set up pots around the garden and hung coloured targets on ropes.

"Can you hit them?" asked the bear. He had rigged some targets so they went up and down.

Zayn started shooting his arrows. His aim got better and better.

"How can we work on avoiding the beams?"
the bear wondered.

"I have just the thing!" Zayn appeared from the shed. "My brother lets me share his tag set."

Zayn loved playing tag so much, he didn't care about the power cut!

And his aim and speed had got much better.

When they had finished training, they fell asleep.

The next day, the bear had disappeared but the power was back on.

Time to reach Level 50!

Zayn tilted his controller this way and that. An arrow flew past the gatekeeper ... and hit the target!

The gate opened and Zayn entered Level 50.
The bear winked.

After reading

Letters and Sounds: Phase 5

Word count: 392

Focus phonemes: /ai/ ay, a-e, ey /ee/ ea /igh/ i-e, i /oa/ o, oe, ow, oul, o-e /oo/ ew, ou, u /ar/ a /ow/ ou /or/ al /ur/ ear, or, ir /e/ ea /oi/ oy /o/ a /air/ ere, ear, are /u/ o, our, o-e

Common exception words: of, to, the, by, my, he, we, me, be, said, have, were, when, are

Curriculum links: Computing; Design and technology; Physical education

National Curriculum learning objectives: Reading/word reading: read accurately by blending the sounds in words that contain the graphemes taught so far, especially recognising alternative sounds for graphemes, read accurately words of two or more syllables that contain the same graphemes as above; Reading/comprehension (KS2): understand what they read, in books they can read independently, by checking that the text makes sense to them, discussing their understanding and explaining the meaning of words in context; making inferences on the basis of what is being said and done

Developing fluency

- Your child may enjoy hearing you read the book.
- Take turns to read a double page. One of you could read Zayn's spoken words, the other the bear's.

Phonic practice

- Focus on the different spellings of the /u/ sound.
- Look at pages 14 and 15. How many words containing the /u/ sound can your child find? (page 14: *come*; page 15: *above*)
- Can they find different spellings of the /u/ sound on pages 19 and 22? (page 19: *u* – **hung**; *our* – **coloured**; page 22: *o* – **wondered**)

Extending vocabulary

- Reread page 12 and focus on the word **sighed**. Discuss what this tells us about how the bear feels. (e.g. *He feels sad or frustrated.*)
- Reread page 13 and discuss what **Zayn's mouth fell open** tells us about his feelings. (e.g. *astonishment, surprise*)
- Can your child think of other ways in which people reveal these feelings? bored (e.g. *yawning*); upset (e.g. *trembling lips*); angry (e.g. *scowling*); scared (e.g. *wide eyes*)